Beau Glenn | Dave Torpley

ASK

Helping Dads and Sons Connect

PURE ADVENTURE PUBLISHING

Being a dad is not about having all the answers.

It's about having the courage to ask the most important questions.

Pure Adventure Publishing
PO Box 101104
Fort Worth Texas 76185
www.pureadventure.org

© 2018 by Beau Glenn
        Dave Tarpley

Printed in the United States of America.

ISBN-13: 978-1-54563-350-2

Dedicated to Men of Courage

How to Use This Book:

ASK HAVE FUN
CLIMB A MOUNTAIN
ROAD TRIP LISTEN
MORNING RIDE TO SCHOOL
FAVORITE MEAL
COUNSEL TAKE A HIKE
SPORTING EVENT
FISHING TRIP ENCOURAGE
KITCHEN TABLE
PLAN IT. MAKE IT HAPPEN.
AFFIRM GET AWAY
JUST SHOW UP.

Small Talk

Us, Part One

Relationships

Us, Part Two

Battles

Us, Part Three

Living Big

Who's Asking?

Dad   Son

"Ask questions from your heart

and you will be answered from the heart."
-Proverb

SMALL TALK

To live big, you have to start small.
Here are some ice-breakers to get
the conversation going.

Events

If you could choose a couple of events to go to, and ticket cost was not a factor, what would the events be (anything – sports, music, art, whatever)?

- Would you want to go with one person or a group of people?
- If one person, who?
- What makes you want to choose that person or that group of people?

- What concert or event do you remember going to?
- Who did you go with, and why?
- Is there anything about high school that brings back positive memories?

Places

Small Talk

Have you ever thought about living in another country?

- If you could choose another country to live in, which would it be?
- Why?

- What's a place you've visited where you could picture yourself living?
- Why would you want to live there?

Bands

Small Talk

Who are your 2-3 favorite bands?

- What do you like about them?
- When you listen to music, do you give more attention to the words or the sound?

- When you were my age, who were your favorite bands?
- Did you and your parents ever listen to music together?
- If so, what did you listen to?

Movies

What are a few of your favorite movies?

- What do you like about them?
- Would you like us to watch one of those movies together? Or maybe some other one?
- If so, would you like to set up a time now?

- Name a few of your favorite movies. What do you like about them?
- Would you like us to watch one of those movies together? Or maybe some other one?
- If so, would you like to set up a time now?

Characters

Small Talk

Could you name a couple of comedians you like?

- What do they do that's funny?
- Any idea how they became popular or famous?

- When you were my age, what were some of your favorite TV shows?
- Why did you like them?
- If you could be a character on TV or in a movie, who would it be? Why?

"Sometimes the question is more

important than the answer."
–Plato

US[1]

The innate bond between father and son isn't just strong –
it stretches in all directions. From childhood memories to
the importance of working together, these are the things
that define who you are and what you mean to each other.

Memories

Us, Part One

What are a couple of favorite memories you have of the two of us being together?

- Why are they special to you?

- What are a couple of good memories you have of our being together?
- Why were they good?

What's Important

Us, Part One

What have you been thinking about that you'd like us to discuss?

- What makes this important to you?

- Is there something you've been hoping we could talk about?
- What makes this important to you?

Crying

Us, Part One

Do you think most guys your age consider crying to be a sign of weakness?

- Why or why not?
- If you don't mind, tell me about a time you cried.

- Do you consider crying to be a sign of weakness or strength?
- Did you ever see your dad cry?
- What kinds of situations make you cry (or want to cry)?

Doing Right

Us, Part One

What am I doing right as a dad in our relationship?

- How can you tell when I'm making an effort to connect with you?

- What am I doing right as your son?
- How can you tell when I'm making an effort to connect with you?

School

Us, Part One

Many kids have negative feelings about school.

- Do you think anything positive might come out of this school year?
- Can you think of anyone you could encourage this year?
- Any ideas of how you could come alongside them?

- Who has supported you when you've felt frustrated at work?
- What did they do to help you?
- Is there someone you are encouraging now, or someone you'd like to encourage?

Acceptance

Us, Part One

When was a time you felt you had to perform (do or say the right things) to get my approval or acceptance?

- What did I do or say that communicated that you needed to earn my approval?
- What have I done recently that made you feel you had to meet my standards?

- Do you remember a time when you felt you couldn't meet someone else's expectations?
- Do you ever feel inadequate or unsure that you can do your job well?

Heroes

Us, Part One

If you could create a superhero, what would he be like?

- In the real world, what makes someone a hero?
- Who do you consider a hero?

- Who is a man you respect?
- What do you like about him?
- Has one of your heroes ever disappointed you?

Independence

In what area(s) of your life do you feel you're ready for more independence?

- Can you give me 1-2 examples of what independence would look like at this stage of your life?
- How can we work together to make this independence real?

- Are there any areas of your life where you feel that something is holding you back?
- If so, what is holding you back?
- What can you do about that?

"Questions are one sure means of turning the focus back to where it belongs – on the people with whom we desire to connect."

-Jedd Medefind & Erik Lokkesmoe

RELATIONSHIPS

In many ways, our lives are defined by the experiences we share with others – whether it's a quirky family tradition or that moment you realize you're falling in love. These experiences and the connections we make are part of what make our lives unique.

Vacations

Relationships

What's a family vacation that you liked?

- What made that vacation memorable?
- Were there any other vacations you liked?

- Tell me about a vacation you took when you were a kid.
- What vacation would you still like to take?

Traditions

Relationships

What was a fun or weird Christmas tradition our family had when you were younger?

- Is there a specific Christmas tradition you would like to start?
- What's good about traditions?

- Are there any traditions we have observed in our family that are an extension of ones you grew up with? If so, which ones?
- If not, is there a tradition you'd like to re-establish from your growing-up years?

Family

Relationships

What do you like about our family?

- Why?
- Is there something we used to do as a family that you miss doing?

- What's something you'd like us to do as a family to draw closer to one another?
- Do you think we have to "walk on eggshells" around anyone in our family? Who?
- Why do you think we walk on eggshells?

Friendships

Men need friends who help them be the best version of themselves and live out their purpose. Friendships based only on pleasure and entertainment are a counterfeit of real friendships and result in loneliness.

- What characteristics do you look for in a friend?
- Is there someone you're friends with now that you hope to still be friends with in ten years?

- Who helps you be the best version of yourself?
- How do they do that?
- Besides a family member, who would you call for help in an emergency?

Serious Relationships

Let's say you're in a serious relationship with a young lady.

- Why might you want to wait to have sex? What are the pros and cons?
- Why might you not want to wait? What are the pros and cons?

- Did you have sex before you got married?
- If you had it to do over again, would you make the same decision? Why or why not?

Living Together

Relationships

Why might a couple want to live together before (or instead of) getting married?

- What are some pros and cons of this choice?

- When talking about relationships, what does commitment mean to you?
- What would you say to me if I chose to live with someone instead of marrying her?

The One

Relationships

Do you think there's one "right" person we're meant to marry?

- Why or why not?
- What are a couple of non-negotiables for the type of person you would want to marry?

- What qualities do you now consider essential in a life partner that didn't seem so important when you were my age?
- When I find the person I want to marry, what role would you like to play during the time leading up to my wedding?

Being Married

Relationships

Besides sex, what do you think you'll like about being married?

- Based on the marriages you've observed, what have you seen that you would like to make part of your own marriage?
- What aspects would you not want to be part of your marriage?

- What kinds of marriage relationships do you admire?
- Knowing me, what kind of person do you think would bring out my strengths and balance out my weaknesses in a marriage relationship?

"The first step to receiving an answer is

**being brave enough
to ask a question."**

-Kaitlyn Bouchillon

US²

The father-son bond is flexible, and sometimes it feels like it's being stretched to its limit. But when you know and understand each other, the tough times don't seem as tough – and the good times are even better.

Being a Dad

What do you want me to keep doing as a dad?

- What do you want me to start doing as your dad?
- What do you want me to stop doing as your dad?

- What's challenging about being a dad?
- What do I do that makes you feel angry? Happy? Proud? Worried?
- What do you hope our relationship will be like by the time I leave for college or move out on my own?

Comparisons

Us, Part Two

It's easy to compare ourselves to others.

- Who do you compare yourself to?
- In what areas do you compare yourself?

- Who do you find yourself playing the comparison- or competition-game with?
- In what areas do you compare yourself?

Getting Away

Us, Part Two

If you and I take off for a weekend, where are a couple of places you'd like to go?

- What are some things you'd like us to do there?
- What are some things you'd rather not do?

- Did you ever get away alone with your dad?
- If so, what kinds of things did you do together?
- If not, what do you wish you had done?

Forgiveness

It's been said that the hardest person to forgive is yourself.

- In what ways do you agree with this?
- In what ways do you disagree?

- What are the pros and cons of forgiving ourselves?
- What are the pros and cons of not forgiving ourselves?
- In what area of your life have you messed up and struggled to forgive yourself?

Autonomy

Being a dad involves my recognizing when it's time for you to start doing certain things for yourself. It's not healthy for me to do some things for you that you can do for yourself.

- When have I tried to take over something that you knew you were capable of doing?
- I want you to realize your strengths and how capable you are. Are you willing to tell me when I'm depriving you of opportunities to do things for yourself?

- What fears do you have about my becoming more independent?
- How can you let go of those fears?
- What do you think I can learn to do for myself to become more independent, including actions, attitudes and insights?

Pressure

Us, Part Two

In what areas of your life are you feeling pressure to do certain things in order to be accepted by a particular person or group?

• What do you want to do about this situation?

• In what areas of your life are you feeling pressure to do certain things in order to be accepted by a particular person or group?

• What do you want to do about this situation?

Other Things

Us, Part Two

What are some things you'd like to know about me?

- What would you like me to know about you?

- What are some things you'd like to know about me?
- What would you like me to know about you?

Love

Us, Part Two

Love can be expressed in a variety of ways.

- What do I do that makes you feel loved by me?
- Talk about a recent time when I showed you love.

- How would you like me to show that I love you?
- When we are fighting or disagreeing with each other, what words do you think we should try not to use?

"Questions are the golden keys that unlock hearts and minds."
-Bob Tiede

Battles

Life is full of conflict – some of it self-inflicted and some out of our control. And the more we endure, the stronger it makes us. But it also helps to have someone to lean on, someone to talk to and provide clarity in confusing and difficult situations.

Challenges

Battles

What's the most challenging thing you've had to overcome?

- What personal skills did you use to make it through the tough time?
- How have you used those skills in other situations?

- When has fear kept you from making it through a tough time?
- What were you afraid of?
- What fears are keeping you from reaching your goals now?

Anger

Battles

Feeling angry is part of being human. People express it in all kinds of ways: yelling, hitting things, pretending it doesn't affect them, talking it out, etc.

- What makes you angry?
- What do you do with your anger?

- What makes you angry?
- What do you do with your anger?

Hope

Battles

Sometimes people lose hope in certain areas of their life.

- Have you ever felt like that?
- Do you feel that way now about anything?

- Have you ever lost hope?
- What have you done to get hope back in your life after losing it?

Doubt

Everyone doubts God at some point in their life.

- Can you remember a time when you've doubted God?

- If so, what were the circumstances?

- How about you? When have you doubted God, and why?

- What did you learn through those experiences?

Guilt

Guilt is a negative emotion we feel when we've done something wrong, while shame is a negative feeling we have about who we are as a person.

- What kinds of things do kids your age feel guilty about?
- How do they deal with their guilt?

- What are some things you feel guilty about?
- Do you ever struggle with shame?

Bitterness

Someone once said that bitterness is like drinking poison and waiting for the other person to die.

- How would you interpret this statement?
- Do you ever feel pushed to say you forgive someone before you're ready?
- How does that make you feel?

- Who have you had trouble forgiving? Why?
- How do you know when you've truly forgiven someone?
- Is it ever a good thing to forgive someone but not forget what they've done?

Drugs

What are some of the most popular drugs with the kids at your school?

- What would motivate you to use drugs, including alcohol?
- What would keep you from using drugs?

- Has drinking and/or using drugs ever been an unmanageable problem for you?
- If so, did you tell anyone about the problem?
- How did they respond?

Pornography

Battles

Some people think that pornography reduces individuals to objects to be used for someone else's pleasure.

- Do you think that's true?
- Why or why not?

- Has pornography ever been a problem for you?
- What did you do or have you done to stop using pornography?
- Some people say pornography can affect a marriage relationship. Do you think that's true?

"A question not asked

is a door not opened."
-Marilee Adams

US³

Keep these questions in mind as you continue to learn about each other – even beyond this book. Honesty is the foundation of any substantive relationship, and the more open you are with these, the more it will cultivate and strengthen that father-son connection.

Criticalness

Am I too critical of you?

- In what areas of your life do I tend to be overly critical?
- How would you like me to approach you about something that concerns me? (I could bring it up while we're sharing a meal, riding in the car, sitting outside on the deck, etc.)

- Are you open to my bringing up issues that bother me about you?
- How would you like me to do that?
- What are 2-3 ground rules we could agree on when bringing up difficult subjects?

Mistakes

Us, Part Three

We all make mistakes and bad decisions sometimes.

- What have you learned from a mistake or poor decision you've made?

- If you could go back and un-make a bad decision, what would it be?
- Have you ever been surprised to see how something good has come from a mistake or bad decision?

Sexual Beings

People want to make sex only about what we do, when in fact sex is more about who we are. We are sexual beings. That's how God created us.

• Does it bother you when I ask you questions about sex?

• If so, how can I make those kinds of conversations less uncomfortable?

• Who or what provided you with information about sex as you were growing to adulthood?

• What do you think are 1-2 misconceptions guys my age have about sex?

Procrastination

What one thing would feel good to get done this week, maybe something you've had on your mind for awhile?

- Is procrastination ever good?

- Have you been putting off something you'd like to get done?
- Can you remember a time you held off doing something, and it ended up paying off?

Stress

Is there anything you're involved with that is causing you to feel stressed out?

- If so, what would you like to do about that?

- What things do you do that tend to increase your stress level?
- What are some ways you avoid feeling overly stressed?

Anger

How do you know when I'm mad?

- Sometimes dads get mad, and their kids think it's their fault.
- Have you ever felt that way? How does it make you feel when you realize that I'm angry?

- How did your dad show his anger?
- What was your typical response to his anger?
- Were there times when you felt that his anger was your fault?

Fear

We're all afraid of something.

- In what kinds of situations can fear be helpful?
- When can it be harmful?

- What are some fears you're facing now?
- Does fear motivate you, or does it stall you out?

Characterize Me

Us, Part Three

Which of the following descriptions would best characterize me as a parent?

- A helicopter dad who constantly rescues you from pain and mistakes
- A drill sergeant who chews you out for making mistakes
- A guide that helps you reach your desired destination

- How will you know when it's best to let me find my own solutions to problems?
- What worries you about the decisions I'm facing now or will face in the near future?

"If I had it to do again, I'd ask more questions

and interrupt
fewer answers."
-Robert Breault

LIVING BIG

We don't know what tomorrow will bring, but exploring options can take us to a future filled with possibilities.

Ambitions

Do you have any dreams/ambitions for your future?

- If so, what actions will help you begin to make progress toward reaching them?
- If not, would you like us to brainstorm and dream together?

- What dreams did you have when you were my age?
- How have your dreams changed through the years?
- Would you give me some examples of actions you've taken to get something you wanted?
- Has anyone helped you achieve a dream?

Money

How much money do you want to save before you leave home?

- What plan will you use to save the money?
- Have you started the plan?
- If not, when do you want to start?
- If so, is your plan working?

- What are a couple of valuable lessons you've learned about money?
- Do you use a plan to save money?
- Do you have a financial planner?
- Why or why not?

Work

Living Big

Would you rather work for a company or own your own business?

- What are some positive aspects of each option?
- If you owned your own business, what are some things you would offer your customers?

- What were some of the jobs you had when you were younger?
- What are some personality strengths that make a person successful in their job?
- Besides personality strengths, what else can help someone excel?

Decisions

What's an important decision you're trying to make right now?

- Why is this important?
- Is there a person you trust who can help you make the decision?
- What makes you trust this person?

- Is there a person you talk to about big decisions in your life? If so, who?
- What decision have you made at work that you feel good about?
- When you are under pressure, how does that affect your ability to make decisions?

Goals

What kinds of things get in the way of reaching the goals you've set for yourself?

- What do you do to get back on track?

- What are some goals you have for yourself?
- What helps you stay focused on specific goals?

Strengths

Everybody has a unique combination of skills, talents and strengths.

- What are yours?
- What can I do to help you further develop in those areas?

- What are your skills, talents and strengths?
- How are you using them to help other people?

Leaders

Living Big

What are some observable (visible) qualities of good leaders?

- What are some internal (less visible) qualities of good leaders?
- Based on your definition of a leader, who among people your age would you consider a leader?
- Why?

- What qualities do you appreciate in good leaders?
- Who had a positive influence on you when you were 16-17 years old?
- What did that person do that made an impact on you?
- Have you ever told them?

The Future

Living Big

As we move toward adulthood, our decisions can have an impact on our future.

- What are 2-3 decisions you're thinking about these days?
- What are some factors you consider when making an important decision?

- Tell me about a decision you've made that has had positive long-term effects.
- What factors do you consider when making an important decision?

"Asking is better than telling."

-Andrew Finlayson

Thank You

Collaboration is just a word until it happens.

We are grateful for the joint efforts of the Balcom Agency's Carol Glover, Audrey Stewart and Jordan Hough. Throughout this project, your professionalism and creativity inspired us.

Cohlby, Melissa, Audra, Jennifer, Mary and Fran of Father & Son Connection, you love and encourage so very well.

Our profound appreciation for the friends and partners of Father & Son Connection and The Landing is immeasurable. Each time someone uses this book, your legacy extends even further.

And Lori Glenn and Heather Tarpley, your willingness to walk with us through the twists and turns of the parenting journey keep giving us the courage to ASK.

–Beau and Dave

Pure Adventure

Pure Adventure is a one-day experience in which fathers and sons meet for a time of fun, outdoor activities, deepened communication and inspirational messages.

Pure Adventure works in preparing a father to fulfill his role as the most significant man in his son's life. Dads and sons dig a little deeper into issues of choosing well, how to have a Christ-like view of women, forgiveness, dealing with physical changes and taming the lion of lust.

- Dads leave Pure Adventure with practical, time-proven tools for staying connected with their sons for a lifetime.

- Boys are equipped and challenged to live their lives as godly men with a proper view of purity and masculinity.

Leadership. Continued.

The Landing

The Landing was created to help ministry leaders and the organizations they serve find solutions rather than live in a problem they have the power to change. Since 1997, The Landing has come alongside leaders in various parts of the United States, Europe and Asia. It is a donor-funded nonprofit leadership organization.

About Beau

Beau Glenn serves as the executive director of Father & Son Connection, which he founded in 2006. As a father and mentor, his passion is that every young man comes to know and experience that he is known, loved, accepted and affirmed by his dad or another man of significant influence.

Over the course of his career, Beau has served as a senior executive and partner in the commercial real estate industry.

Beau received a bachelor of business administration in finance. He and his wife Lori have four children.

About Dave

Dave Tarpley is the creator of Pause and Effect Coaching and co-founder of The Landing, a clergy-support nonprofit. Drawing on more than 20 years of experience as a leadership coach and recovering addict, Dave shows individuals practical ways to translate thinking into action for moving forward.

Over the years, Dave's writing, teaching and consulting have helped leaders in the health care, education, nonprofit, manufacturing and financial services industries.

Dave holds a master's degree in counselor education. He and his wife Heather are the parents of three adult children.

CPSIA information can be obtained
at www.ICGtesting.com
Printed in the USA
BVHW02s2150251018
531243BV00007B/9/P

9 781545 633502